Salvo Spedale Sommelier

HOW TO TASTE THE WINE
Practical manual to learn step by step the techniques of wine tasting

Presentation

History and passion, territory and traditions, sensations and emotions: there is all of this in a glass of wine.

Unpredictable and full of surprises, the wine wins anyone tries to know it deeply. It rewards their commitment showing the best sides of their nature.

Learning to taste means assaying the wine with attention, connecting the sensations perceived at its history and its evolution, expressing a conditioning valuation as little as possible by personal tastes.

Simply and linear, this manual gives the instruments to approach the wine world from the main door, interpreting the sensations and speaking about them with a synthetic but exhaustive and effective language. It will be the personal experience, the passion and the deepening that allows to become expert and competent tasters.

Salvo Spedale

President of Assovini
Director of Panel Assovini Sommelier
Sommelier AIS

ASSOVINI (National Association of Wine Producers and Wine Tourism)
www.assovini.it - The Portal of Wine and Wineries
www.assovini.com - The 1° didactic E-commerce of Wine

Assovini

ORGANOLEPTIC ANALYSIS OF WINE

- **Visual analysis - Introduction**
  - Visual analysis: what is evacuate

- **Olfactory analysis - Introduction**
  - The olfaction: how the perfumes arrive
  - The perfumes
  - The perfumes nature
  - The families
  - The olfactory valuation: how it is performed
  - The olfactory valuation: what is evaluated
  - Correspondence table between types of wine and aromas

- **Taste-olfactory exam - Introduction**
  - The tongue
  - The taste evaluation: how it is performed
  - The taste evaluation: what is evaluated

FINAL CONSIDERATIONS

- **Evolution state**

- **Overall harmony**

- **Olfactory scents of wine**

- **Serving temperature of the wine**

- **Examples of technical tastes of the wine**

VISUAL ANALYSIS - INTRODUCTION

The visual exam is the first step of the organoleptic analysis and it allows to acquire a series of information in order to understand the type of wine, its composition and its evolution.

These information often bring back at many differences, that usually are related to the territory of production and especially to the pedoclimatic ambient, the vine and the production techniques.

The judgement criteria object of the visual exam are: Clarity, Colour and Consistence of wine; instead, if the analysis concerns a sparkling wine, in substitution of the consistence, the effervescence will be evaluated.

Furthermore, it has to be taken into account that the visual exam can give rise to negative results like alterations or diseases, frustrating the rest of the taste, but using the modern technologies allows to make these situations rare.

VISUAL EVALUATION:

1. CLARITY

This exam is done in order to make sure that the wine isn't affected by alterations or diseases. In that case, it has to be taken into account that the most aged wines can present a relative grade of degree.

The clearness of the wine is conditioned by the presence of any particles in suspension, indicating possible defects, while transparency is given by the colouring substances in the wine, whose quantities, filtered by luminous rays, give possibility to identify wines that are poor in colouring substances, like white wine, or rich of colouring substances, like the red ones.

To perform this exam, it's sufficient to place the wine glass between the eye and a light source, for example a candle.

According to the degree of clearness, wine can be defined:

• **Veiled:** high presence of particles in suspension, probably due to alterations or diseases;

• **Quite clear:** minimal presence of veiling, usually due to refermentation or long aging;

• **Clear:** free by any particles; it can be verified by positioning a wine glass on a text, it must be readable to prove it;

• **Crystal clear:** absence of particles in suspension and relevant brightness.

• **Brilliant:** shining limpidity which reflect the luminous rays with vivacity.

2. COLOUR

Polyphenolic substances like anthocyanins, flavones, catechins, acids, etc., contained mainly in the peel, determine the colour of the wine.

To obtain coloured wines it is necessary to have a contact, that is maceration, between the liquid component, the must, and the solid one, that is the peel of the grapes.
Thus the vinification in red takes place, allowing to obtain red and rose wines, according to the quantity of colouring substances in the peels, to the temperature, to the maceration time and to other components that determine the extraction.
Instead, by eliminating the peels from the pomace, the vinification in white takes place, allowing to obtain white wines.

The colour evaluation is performed in order to verify both if any possible defects are present and the correspondence with its type, its relation with the production area, especially with the pedoclimatic area, the vine and its potential of evolution.

Colour characteristics:

• **Intensity**: The quantity of colouring substances determines the colour intensity of wine. They arise from both permanent factors of the pedoclimatic environment (place, latitude, exposition, microclimate, soil) and variable factors (vine, seasonal trend of precipitations, maturation of the grapes, vinification techniques, etc.)

• **Shade**: The type of pigmentation in the wine, the acidity, the pH and the oxidation state of polyphenolic substances determine the colour shade.

The colour shade gives information about the vine used in the wine production and its evolution state.
• **Vivacity**: The vivacity of a wine is a decisive factor because it represents its health conditions, whose depends by the used grape, by the vinification techniques and by the conservation in appropriate places.

The wine colour must be evaluated at the centre of the glass, while the eventual reflection (trend) is found on the nail, that is the tightest part of liquid, formed by inclining the glass.

WHITE WINE COLOURS

• **Greenish yellow.** The wine has a tender yellow colour, with greenish reflections that have the tendency of assuage during the evolution. This colour

is usually found in young and crisp wines, obtained with a slightly early harvest, in which the acid prevails over the softness.

• **Pale yellow.** Similar at the colour of the straw, these wines are young and they are obtained from aged grapes with a balance between acidity and softness.

• **Golden yellow.** Recalling the golden yellow colour, these wines are obtained from a lightly over-aged grapes or matured in barrel grapes, in which the softness prevails over the acidity. If vivacity is missing, probably it's due to oxidation.

• **Amber yellow.** This colour reminds the topaz stone, whose amber colour suggests that these wines are obtained from a late harvest, in which raisins and liquored wines are produced.

About them, due to the high sugar content, the properties of softness definitely prevail over the acidity.

ROSE WINE COLOURS

• **Pale pink.** Shade of colour that reminds the peach blossom or the rose petals of the same-named colour. The wines taking this colour are usually obtained from black grapes, submitted to a short maceration of the peel in contact with the must.

• **Cherry pink.** Shade of rose wines that have a more intense colour than pale pink ones. The cherry pink colour is usually given by black grapes submitted to a lightly longer maceration than the previous case.

• **Clear pink.** Shade of colour typical of rose wines that have a more similar colour to the red ones. These wines are obviously obtained from black grapes submitted to a even longer maceration than the two previous cases.

RED WINE COLOURS

• **Purplish red.** Bright ruby red shade with purple reflections, reminding the fuchsia pink colour or the cardinal's robes. This shade is typical of very young wines with a strong predominance of hard parts (acidity and tannicity).

• **Ruby red.** Shade of red recalling the same-named stone and that can found in quite young red wines, whose, as well as appear in an excellent healthy state, are characterised by good balance between hard and soft parts, for which they're ready to be consumed.

• **Garnet red.** Shade of colour that can be found in sophisticated red wines, usually submitted to aging, presenting softness characteristics that prevail over

the hardnesses. The depth of this colour might indicate a good compactness, if it recalls the red blood colour, otherwise the pomegranate red, if it's more transparent.

• **Orange red.** Shade recalling the bricks colour with reflections from brown to orange. This colour is usually found in long aged wines and they are characterised by a good softness.

However, if this shade turns out dull or if it's found in young wines, it would be considered negatively, because we might be In presence of an early evolution or a degradation caused by an oxidation.

3. CONSISTENCE

The analysis of the consistence of the wine allows to gain useful information about the richness of ethyl alcohol and extractive substances, allowing to verify the correspondence to the typology.

The wine is made up of water (~85%), alcohol (9÷13%) and other components (~3%). A higher or lower presence of all the substances (especially ethanol and glycerol) will ensure that they flow on each other, making the product assume a variable aspect from fluid to viscous.

This exam is made up of two steps:

• By observing the taproom while pouring the wine, that can descend in the glass in a light or oily;

• By observing tears and tensional arches while inclining the glass of 45° or shaking the wine, creating the "tears" and the arches, that are more or less regular curves, formed due to the higher or lower presence of alcoholics components.

By rotating the glass, ethylic alcohol tends to evaporate, increasing the density of the liquid falling to the bottom. If ethanol is predominant over glycerol, dense arches are observed, otherwise they are larger.

According to the consistence, wine can be defined:

• **Fluid:** It's a wine descending through the glass in a too light way, with fast tears and large arches, that's means structural weakness. Negative situation;

• **Not much consistent:** The wine descends through the glass in a quite light way, with fast tears and large arches. It's a verifiable situation in wines that have prevailing characteristics of hardness, low content of ethylic alcohol and structure weaknesses;

• **Quite consistent:** This rating is reserved to wines descending through the glass with moderate fluency, showing a quite equilibrated balance between hardness and softness;

• **Consistent:** A consistent wine descends through the glass in a less fluency way, showing a prevalence of softnesses. It can be verified if regular and dense arches are formed;

• **Viscous:** A viscous wine has syrupy characteristics, revealed by the formation of dense arches and very slow tears. This situation happens in a very few dessert wines. Otherwise, if this happens in other typologies of wine, it would be considered an anomaly probably caused by the racy.

4. EFFERVESCENCE

The effervescence is an evaluation parameter reserved to sparkling wines, characterized by the presence of the fizzle and carbon dioxide, that forms the bubbles.

The characteristic "perlage" represents a good thing in young white wines, because of the action that it plays towards the acidity, while it becomes negative if it's formed after the alcoholic fermentation, that is the case of aged red wines.

The elements of evaluation of the bubbles are:
• **The dough of the bubbles that can be:**
◦ **Gross, if they recalls mineral water;**
◦ **Quite fine**, if they are of standard size;
◦ **Fine**, similar to pin holes.

• **Number of bubbles that can be:**
◦ **Lower**, if almost missing;
◦ **Quite numerous**, if they appear in a discontinuous and scattered way;
◦ **Numerous**, if they are abundant.

• **Persistence of the bubbles, that can result:**
◦ **Evanescents**, if they quickly disappear;
◦ **Quite persisting**, if they disappear after several minutes;
◦ **Persisting**, if they continue to quickly form even after being a long time in the glass.

OLFACTORY EXAM

The olfactory exam is the second step of the taste and it serves to find out and describe the odorous background of wine.

This step is useful to find any defects caused by external factors of wine (mould, cup, scum) but more importantly to verify any particularities due from the wine typology, that are the production place, the vine, the age, etc.

THE OLFACTION – HOW THE PERFUMES ARRIVES

The perfumes are volatile substances that have smell and have the capacity to evaporate, forming the wine bouquet.

The nose apparatus, which have a 10.000 times superior sensorial capacity than the gustatory organs, is the predisposed organs to analyse the various perfumes. The smell perception takes place thanks to the olfactive lining – made up of a cellular stratum equipped of terminal eyelashes – that recognises the sensations and sends them to the cerebral olfactive centres.

Among all the sensitive organs employed in wine tasting, olfactory is our most active mechanical/chemical sense: in the inhalation, the odorous compounds arrive at the linings to be identified.

There are two main canals:

- **Nasal direct way:**

◦ By diffusion, when the odorous particles mix with the air entering through the nose;
◦ Through vortex currents, when we brusquely inspire and the odorous particles attach themselves to the olfactive lining; this is the most effective method in the tasting step in order to reach the nasal cavities;

- **Retro-nasal way**:

◦ Conventionally, by swallowing some liquid, hot air goes out pushed by the throat and it meets the just inhaled cold air; this olfactive sensation is called **"mouth aroma"** or "Intense aromatic persistence" (I.A.P).

THE PERFUMES

Perfumes and/or aromas are unleashed by "volatile" substances, that are capable of evaporating from the liquid part.

The vine characteristics, the production steps, the wine maturation are the factors which confer about 200 odorous compounds belonged to different groups like alcohol, fatty acids, aldehydes, ketones, esters, ethers, terpenes and others too.

The wine recognition happens not according to their chemical nomenclature, but identifying them with the present fragrances in nature (flowers, fruits, spices, etc.).

The reason why chemical names are translated is because they would be too complex and less enjoyable compared to familiar expressions connected to the world nature. On the other hand, it's easy to understand how it would be more enjoyable using expressions like "honey", or "rose" instead of the definitions "phenylethyl acid" or "phenylethyl alcohol".

THE PERFUMES NATURE

The odorous background of the wine can be classified in three groups of perfumes:

Primary perfumes (varietal aromas). This typology of perfumes derives from the vine in which wine has been obtained. Odorous perceptions of moss, sage, rose and other flowers and fruits are often related to the terpenes characterizing the wine fragrance. Perfumed sensations perceived in moscato, malvasia, brachetto and gewürztraminer are those that stand out a marked aromaticity.

Secondary perfumes (fermentation aromas). Secondary perfumes are formed during the process of aging, that is the pre-fermentative step, which means before the starting of fermentation, including pressing, and post-fermentative steps too, during the alcoholic and malolactic fermentation.

Tertiary perfumes(aging bouquets). Tertiary perfumes derive from maturation and refinement of the wine in barrel and they are formed with the slow flowing of the time, while acids, tannins and other components are involved in processes of redox and chemical reactions that bring to the formation of the odorous bouquet.

OLFACTORY EVALUATION: HOW IT IS PERFOMED

In order to correctly perform the olfactory exam, it's necessary to grip the glass rapier, on the base or on the stem, as far away as possible from the mouth, in order to prevent contaminations between the wine perfumes and the smells issued from the hand.

Then it's necessary to follow three steps:

Step 1. The glass must be moved near to the nose and then it's necessary to inspire at regular intervals, with correct stops, in order to avoid habituations to the perfumes;

Step 2. The glass must be slowly rotated creating the ""wine funnels" and let the odorous substances unleash, then we intensively inspire; then we must rotate the glass more intensively and frequently inspire at regular intervals;

Step 3. The wine must be tasted by swallowing and finally, exhaling, the "mouth aroma" is created, bringing back to the olfactive lining the other scents freed because of the body temperature (36-37°C).

OLFACTORY EVALUATION

1. INTENSITY. The intensity of perfumes and/or aromas is a vertical olfactive aspect because sensations are added and perceived at the same time.

According to the olfactive intensity, a wine can be defined as:

• **Lacking,** Very few odorous sensations;

• **Not very intense,** limited odorous sensations;

• **Quite intense,** Quite perceptible odorous sensations;

• **Intense,** Definitively perceptible odorous sensations;

• **Very intense,** Very intense and marked odorous sensations.

2. COMPLEXITY. The complexity of aromas is an horizontal olfactive aspect because the amount of sensations follow each other without overlapping, causing a certain persistence of the perfumes.

According to the complexity, a wine can be defined as:

• **Lacking,** Very few successions of perfumes;

• **Not very complex,** Few successions of perfumes;

• **Quite complex,** sufficient successions of perfumes;

• **Complex,** durable successions of perfumes;

• **Ample,** prolonged and complex successions of perfumes, they continue for even minutes.

3. QUALITY. It's a subjective evaluation in the taste that define the outline of intensity and complexity. In this sense, the taster has to avoid influences from his personal tastes, that are irrelevant in the analysis of the objective quality of the product.

According to the olfactive quality, a wine can be defined as:

• **Common**, bad perfume, poor of quality;

• **Poorly fine**, Almost mediocre;

• **Quite fine**, sufficiently fine and enjoyable;

• **Fine**, enjoyable, distinct, fresh, balanced;

• **Excellent**, particularly enjoyable, distinct, fresh.

4. DESCRIPTION OF THE PERFUME OF THE WINE

Thanks to the olfactory sense, it's possible to give a qualitative anf quantitative description of the characteristics of a wine.

The definitions are:

• *Aromatic.* It brings back to the aromatic components of the vine (Moscato, Malvasia, Brachetto, Gewürztraminer, etc.).

• *Vinous.* It can be found mainly in young red wines and it recalls the vinification steps (most, pomace, winery).

• *Floreal.* In white young wines it recalls scents of white flowers, while in less young red wines it recalls scents of red flowers.

• *Fruity.* It recalls different varieties of fruit typically with red pulp in red wines and with white pulp in white wines.

• *Fragrant.* It's a perfume that is definitively attributable at the wine typology usually recalling floral and fruity scents mixed to the bread crust aroma.

• *Herbaceous.* It recalls scents of green vegetables and chopped grass.

• *Mineral.* It's related to mineral and saline odorous sensations like flintstones, hydrocarbons, gunpowder, graphite, slate.

• *Spicy.* It's a perfume that can be attributed at spice scents and it's usually found in red and white wines that are matured in barrel and refined in bottle.

• *Roasted.* Perfume derived from the evolution of the wines, especially after the maturation in new barriques.

• ***Ethereal.*** It's a perfume included in the bouquet of the wine, which means that it derives from the different steps of wide aging. It's a perfume that collects different sensations deriving from primary, secondary and tertiary aromas evolved through the time.

CORRESPONDANCE TABLE BETWEEN WINE TYPES AND AROMAS

• FLOWERS
◦ *BROOM = evolved white wines*
◦ *HAWTHORN = delicate scent*
◦ *VIOLET = Barbaresco*

• FRUITS
◦ *GRAPEFRUIT = sauvignon blanc*
◦ *GREEN APPLE = harsh scent, pungent*
◦ *WHITE PLUM = sylvaner*
◦ *RIBES/CASSIS = black pinot , Cabernet Sauvignon*
◦ *ANANAS = Chardonnay, late harvest*
◦ *PEAR = Sparkling wine, Sauternes*
◦ *BLACKBERRY = Syrah, Dolcetto d'Alba*
◦ *STRAWBERRY = Barbaresco, Cannonau*
◦ *STRAWBERRY = Young wines, black pinot , cabernet franc, zinfandel*
◦ *CHERRY = Classic Chianti*
◦ *WILD BERRIES = teroldego*

• DRY FRUITS
◦ *ALMOND = cabernet sauvignon*

• JAM
◦ *BLOSSOM HONEY = evolved citrus wine*
◦ *HONEY = Sauternes*

• SPICES
◦ *CARDAMOM = gaglioppo*
◦ *LICORICE = merlot, pinot nero*
◦ *VANILLA = wines that are passed in barrique*
◦ *BLACK PEPPER = syrah, cabernet franc, cabernet sauvignon, barolo, barbaresco*

• ROASTED
◦ *FUME' = Barolo, Brunello (From the terrain, and not from the wood)*

• HERBACEOUS / AROMATIC

- *SAGE = sauvignon blanc*
- *FRESH THYME = sauvignon blanc*
- *MOSS = black pinot*
- *UNDERBRUSH = black pinot*
- *YELLOW PEPPER = sauvignon blanc*
- *GREEN PEPPER = cabernet franc*
- *TRUFFLE = cabernet sauvignon, barolo, Brunello*
- *TOMATO LEAF = sauvignon blanc*

- **ETHEREAL**
- *GLAZE = Lagrein*

TASTE – OLFACTORY EXAM

This final step of the sensorial analysis takes into account a greater number of parameters and it's useful for the verify and the synthesis of what emerged in the previous visual and olfactive exams. In fact, previous obtained data can be confirmed or not by the taste – olfactory analysis.

The sense of taste give us the following sensations:

FLAVOR SENSATIONS

The principal flavours are 4:

• **Sweetness,** (sugar/alcohol): this sensation, perceived on the tongue tip, gives gustative enjoyment, because of the presence of sugar residues;

• **acidity,** it's a less enjoyable sensation, perceived on the anterior lateral parts of the tongue and it's due to the acids that are present in the wine, causing salivation;

• **sapidity,** it's a pleasant sensation of flavour perceived on the posterior lateral zones of the tongue, caused by the presence of mineral salts;

• **bitterness,** it's a not very pleasant sensation perceived in the posterior zone of the tongue, due to the presence of polyphenols, especially tannins. If the bitter sensation is too intense, it could be an anomaly which is part of the defects of the wine.

TACTILE SENSATIONS

• **Thermal.** It's a sensation that is attributable to the service temperature of the wine. Depending on the thermic condition, flavour sensations change with the

changing of the temperature, for which higher values bring to softness sensations, while lower values favour perceptions of sapidity and bitterness. Also the acidity, even if not directly influenced by the temperature changes, causes acid perceptions obviously, but by increasing the temperature it's possible to mitigate this perception, whose effect fuels the pseudo-caloric perception of sweetness and softness.

• **Softness.** The pleasant sensation of softness, that can be found in a velvet and wrapping wine, is caused by polyalcohols, especially by glycerine, ethylic alcohol, eventual sugar residues and other substances. An example of softness could be given by a piece of butter slowly loosened in the mouth.

• **Astringency.** A typical sensation of astringency can be found in young red wines, whose tannins are principal factors of roughness perceptions and of the sense of dry in the mouth. Examples of this tactile perception could be the taste of raw artichokes or unripe pears.

• **Pungency.** This tactile sensation is due to the typical tingling produced by carbon dioxide saturated bubbles in the mouth when we taste a semi-sparkling wine or a sparkling wine.

• **Gustative consistency.** It's the typical sensation of gustative fullness that come from a wine that is particularly rich of extracts. The analysis allows to determine in the details if the consistency perception derives from the type of substance, that is aqueous, fluid or viscous.

RETRONASAL SENSATIONS (MOUTH AROMA)

The typical retronasal sensation is produced from the contact between the hot air pushed from the pharynx, produced after the deglutition of a liquid, and the just inhaled cold air; this taste-olfactive sensation is called "**mouth aroma**" or "Intense Aromatic Persistence".

THE TONGUE
The tongue is the principal organ of the taste, it's made up of a muscle that is covered by a membrane that contains tiny protuberances, that are the taste buds, that have various forms and dimensions.

The tongue not only communicates the perceptions of the various flavors at the brain, but also makes easier the mastication of food, while the taste buds perceive the four fundamental flavours, that are:

• **SWEET:** sensation that is perceived on the tongue tip, in which there are the fungiform papillae;

• **BITTER:** sensation that is perceived on the dorsal zone of the tongue, in which there are the circumvallate papillae;

• **SALTY:** sensation that is perceived on the lateral posterior zones of the tongue;

• **ACID:** sensation that is perceived on the lateral anterior zones of the tongue.

Furthermore, in the central dorsal zone there are also the filiform papillae that have a tactile function, in fact they recognise the different consistency of the liquids and solids entering the mouth.

TASTE-OLFACTORY EVALUATION: HOW IT IS PERFORMED

• **Step 1.** First, we need to make a primary approach of the mouth, introducing a low quantity of wine, in order to prepare the oral cavity for the technical taste.

• **Step 2**. A second low quantity of wine must be introduced, thus beginning the tasting.

• **Step 3.** The wine must be brought in the anterior zone of the mouth, then we must inspire making the liquid expand in the entire oral cavity, allowing a larger extension of the gustative sensations.

• **Step 4.** While slowly exhaling, the tongue will favour the impact with the entire oral cavity, allowing to evaluate the balance of all the different components: sugar, alcohols, acids, tannins;

Then we must swallow and exhale while chewing with the empty mouth. This step produces the mouth aroma that makes possible to evaluate the Intense Aromatic Persistence, both olfactive and gustative.

GUSTATIVE EVALUATION: WHAT IS EVALUATED

1. SOFTNESS

a. SUGAR. Glucose and Fructose, but also sucrose and maltose, are very important substances in the composition of wine, because they produce the sweetness sensation. These types of sugar are present in every type of fruit, and it's present in a quantity about 150-250 g/Kg in the grape.

• **Dry,** Low or absent sensation of sweetness;

• **Semisweet,** Very low sensation of sweetness;

• **Lovely,** Clear sensation of sweetness;

• **Sweet,** predominant sensation of sweetness;

• **Fulsome,** Too high sensation of sweetness. Negatively evaluated.

During the alcoholic fermentation of the must, the action of the lees on the sugar starts the production of ethylic alcohol, carbon dioxide and other secondary substances. However, from not completely transformed we can obtain a more or less sweet wine.
According to the quantity of sugar and to the perception of sweetness, a wine can be defined as:

b. ALCOHOLS. After water, (75-80%), alcohols, from which ethylic, methylic, propylic, etc., are the most present elements in the wine (4-20%), that are formed in the alcoholic fermentation.

From these, the ethanol is the one who produces the pseudocalorica effect perceived during the taste of an alcoholic drink. It not only express the alcoholic graduation of the wine, but also it contribute at making it softer, mitigating the hardness of acids, tannins and mineral salts.

According to the alcoholic perception, a wine can be defined as:

• **Soft,** low or absent pseudocalorica sensation (4-7°)

• **Not very hot,** moderate pseudocalorica sensation (10-11°)

• **Quite hot,** strong pseudocalorica sensation, (11-12°, situation of balance with the other components)

• **Hot,** Very strong pseudocalorica sensation (12-13,5°)

• **Alcoholic** predominant pseudocalorica sensation (15-18°, typical of liqueur wines).

c. POLYALCOHOLS. During the alcoholic fermentation of the must, the action of the lees on the sugar starts the production of ethylic alcohol, carbon dioxide and other secondary substances. However, from not completely transformed we can obtain a more or less sweet wine.

According to the quantity of sugar and to the perception of sweetness, a wine can be defined as:

• **Edgy strong absence of softness, defective wine.**

• **Not very soft** Low sensation of softness, young wines.

• **Quite soft** enjoyable sensation of softness, young, ready and structured wines.

• **Soft** strong sensation of softness, matured and structured wines.

• **Mellow** predominant sensation of softness (typical of white dessert wines).

2. HARDNESS

- **ACIDS.** The acids are components of the wine that determine an important aspect of the flavour, giving it a sensation of freshness.

They are distinguished in:

• **organic of pre-fermentation** (tartaric, malic, citric fixed) and organic of post-fermentation (lactic, succinic fixed; acetic, propionic volatile);

• **inorganic of post-fermentation** and sulphuric, phosphoric and hydrochloric salts.

The acid strength is measured by the pH (in the wine it's usually between 3,1 and 3,7). The penetration strength is the one that the wine has against the taste buds.
According to the acid perception, a wine can be defined as:

• *Flat* Poor of acidity (too aged or diseased wine).

• *Not very fresh* low sensation of acidity (matured wine).

• *Quite fresh* good sensation of acidity, it procures a certain salivation (young red and white wine, more evolved rose wines).
• *Fresh,* good sensation of acidity, it procures an abundant salivation (white and semi-sparkling rose wines, sparkling wines).

• *Acidulous,* predominant sensation of acidity (not matured wines).

   b. TANNINS. The category that include polyphenols is made up principally by tannins and pigments, present in the grape seeds and in the skin of the grapes.

While the pigments characterize the wine colour, tannins determine the tannicity of red wines (and some types of white wines), perceivable in the palate with sensations of rugosity, astringency, sense of dry and sometimes with a soft bitter sensation.

According to the degree of tannic perception, a wine can be defined as:

   • *Squashy,* low presence of tannic components, aged or altered wine.

   • *Not very tannic,* very low tannic sensation, typical of young wines, clarets or aged red wines.

   • *Quite tannic,* Sufficient tannic sensation that can be found in red wines of average/great structure.

   • *Tannic,* strong tannic sensation typical of young red wines.

• ***Astringent,*** predominant tannic sensation that stops the secretion of saliva.

c. *MINERAL SALTS.* The sapidity is a gustative micro-sensation attributable at different groups of mineral substances, like anions of organic or inorganic acids, metals, potassium, etc. present in the wine.
The presence of mineral salts in the wine is variable due to various factors, like the pedoclimatic ambient, the different wine-making processes, the conservation and the refinement.

According to the degree of sapidity, a wine can be defined as:

• **Prosy,** lack of mineral sensations, typical of aged wines or wines obtained from bad grapes.

• **Not very sapid,** low mineral sensations.

• **Quite sapid,** balanced fresh/sapid sensations.

• **Sapid,** enjoyable salt sensation, wine obtained from grapes of warm areas.

• **Salty,** predominant salt sensation, wines of swampy areas.

3. STRUCTURE OR BODY OF THE WINE

The non-volatile components of the wine, like fixed acids, sugar, polyphenols, salts, glycerine, etc. extracted from the water, form the dry extract, determining the structure or body of the wine. In white wines, the dry extract is usually between 16/22 g/l, while in red wines between 20/30 g/l.

According to the structure, a wine can be defined as:

• ***Thin***, abnormal and insufficient structure, wines obtained from wrong productions or damaged grapes.

• ***Weak***, modest structure, wines that must be drunk when they're young.

• ***Full-bodied***, good structure, obtained in syntony with the type of grapes and their degree of maturation.

• ***Robust***, well-structured and balanced, great or particular wines.

• ***Heavy***, too much structure, wines bad processed or wines that still need some aging.

4.1 GUSTATIVE BALANCE

The softnesses (sugar, alcohols, polyalcohols), that procures delicate sensations, and the hardnesses (acids, tannins, mineral salts), characterized by more aggressive sensations, should be always in balance, not prevailing on each other, in order to make the wine appreciated for his gustative enjoinment.

According to the gustative balance, a wine can be defined as:

• ***Not very equilibrated,*** if one of the two sensation prevail over the other.

• ***Quite equilibrated,*** if one of the two sensations doesn't hardly prevail over the other.

• ***Equilibrated,*** if there is the correct balance between the two sensations, according to the typology of wine.

4.2 TASTE-OLFACTIVE INSENSITY

The taste-olfactory intensity is a difference related to the impact that all the substances determining the wine flavour exercise at the same time over the taste buds and the receptors present in the tongue and in the oral mucosa. It's made up of the elements giving structure, the ethylic alcohol and the aromatic substances.

According to the taste-olfactive intensity, a wine can be defined as:

• ***Lacking,*** very low gustative and taste/olfactive sensations.

• ***Not very intense,*** reduced gustative and taste/olfactive sensations.

• ***Quite intense,*** balanced gustative and taste/olfactive sensations.

• ***Intense,*** good gustative and taste/olfactive sensations.

• ***Very intense,*** deep gustative and taste/olfactive sensations.

4.3 GUSTATIVE PERSISTENCE

The taste/olfactive persistence, or intense aromatic persistence, is made up of the combination of the sensations remaining after the deglutition and the exhaling and that goes away more or less slowly.

According to the gustative persistence, a wine can be defined as:

• **Short,** perception < 2 seconds.

• **Not very persistent,** perception between 2 - 4 seconds.

• **Quite persistent,** perception between 4 - 6 seconds.

• **Persistent,** perception between 6 - 8 seconds.

• **Very persistent,** perception > 8 seconds.

4.4 GUSTATIVE QUALITY

Intensity and taste/olfactive persistence, as well as elegance, finesse and typicity, are the characteristics that allow to express a judgement about the gustative quality of the wine.

Like for olfactive quality, object of study during the olfactory exam, this step too gives an important role to the subjectivity of the taster, that must be intended as his wealth of experience of the wine tasted through the time, not as the influence of his personal tastes.

According to the gustative quality, a wine can be defined as:

• *Common,* bad wine.

• *Not very smooth,* poor wine, normal flavour.

• *Quite smooth,* sufficiently smooth, good flavour.

• *Smooth*, good wine, balanced, elegant flavour.

• *Excellent,* distinct wine, rich and complex flavour.

FINAL CONSIDERATIONS

Once completed the three steps of the sensorial analysis (visual, olfactive, gustative) it's possible to draw conclusions about two final aspects.

EVOLUTIVE STATE

The evolutive state of the wine represents his quality in function of the evolution through the time, that be compared with the life steps of the man: at the beginning it's not mature, but it grows until it becomes old. Every type of wine, with different modalities and times, runs through this evolutive grown that, for some wines, takes a few months, while for others it has a more durative grown, that takes some years or some decades.

Anyway, the evaluations must take into accounts that some wines reach the maximum quality expression only in the maturation, while other wines only if they remains young.

According to the evolutive state, a wine can be defined as:

• *Not mature,* wine with different anomalous situations, it still has to mature/refine.

• *Young,* not balanced but enjoyable situations, it can potentially improve with maturation/refinement

• *Ready,* still in evolution but appreciable (majority of the wines in commerce)

• *Mature,* optimal harmony, maximum degree of appreciation.

• *Old,* failure of the characteristics (variations of the colors, reduction/alteration of the aromas, flattening of the flavour).

COMPLESSIVE HARMONY

The harmony is the synthesis of the result of the sensorial analysis of the wine, given by the coherence of the characteristics in the different steps of the taste, together with an elevate quality level.

According to the harmony, a wine can be defined as:

• **Not very harmonic,** strong discrepancy between the components that are responsible of the organoleptic characteristics.

• **Quite harmonic,** some imperfection in one or more components that are responsible of the organoleptic characteristics.

• **Harmonic,** perfect combination of the components that are responsible of the organoleptic characteristics.

OLFACTIVE SCENTS OF THE WINE

The perfume of a wine is usually given by the result of a combination that will have to result enjoyable and harmonious. The scents of freshness are most perceptible in young wines, while in more evolved wines the scents of longevity prevail.

• **Young White wine**
  ◦ white and yellow fresh flowers
  ◦ fruits with white pulp
  ◦ aromatic herbs
  ◦ vegetal scents
  ◦ mineral scents

• **Evolved White wine**
  ◦ yellow flowers
  ◦ exotic matured fruits and fruits with yellow pulp
  ◦ jam of fruits with white and yellow pulp
  ◦ candied and dry fruits
  ◦ spices and roasted scents

• **Young Red wine**
  ◦ purple and red fresh flowers
  ◦ fruits with red and black berry
  ◦ vegetal scents
  ◦ mineral scents

• **Evolved Red wine**

◦ purple and red withered flowers
◦ jam of fruits with black and red berry
◦ dry fruits
◦ spices
◦ roasted scents
◦ animal scents
◦ ethereal scents

SERVICE TEMPERATURES OF THE WINE

• Dry Sparkling wines **4-6 °C**
• Sweet Sparkling wines and Semi-sparkling wines **6-8 °C**
• Young white wines and rose wines **8-10 °C**
• Young structured wines, passito and white liqueur wines **10-12 °C**
• Structures rose wines, delicate and not very tannic red wines **12-14 °C**
• Middle structured and tannic red wines, passito and red liqueur wines **14-16 °C**
• Evolved red wines, with great structure and tannicity **16-18 °C**

EXAMPLES OF WINE TASTING

Denomination: Cannonau Rosso Riserva
Typology: Red
Region: Sardinia
Degustation: the Cannonau Riserva is a wine that has a red colour tending to garnet with the aging; it has a floral perfume of rose or dry petal, fruited from matured fruits (jam and dry plum) with a spiced (cloves and cinnamon-vanilla) and vegetal from balsamic (mentholated – eucalyptol) background; the flavour is characteristic, dry, sapid, full, very warm, soft, bitter aftertaste, softly tannic.

Denomination: Verdicchio dei Castelli di Jesi
Typology: White
Region: Marche
Degustation: the Verdicchio is a structured wine, full-bodied and elegant; it presents itself with a pale yellow colour, with evident greenish reflections that reveal its fragrance, vivacity and a certain freshness. Strong are the perfumes of hawthorn and wildflowers, while in the palate it's perceived fresh fruits of peach, apple with soft citrus points and an aftertaste of bitter almond.

Denomination: Lago di Caldaro
Typology: Red
Region: Trentino Alto Adige
Degustation: the Lago di Caldaro is a red coloured wine that is characterized by fruited aromas with scents of cherry, raspberry, bitter almond and violet. It's a dry and structured wine, with soft tannins and an enjoyable degree of acidity. Stimulant and easy to drink, it's suitable to be drunk in all the occasions.

Denomination: Prosecco
Typology: White Sparkling Wine
Region: Veneto

Degustation: the Prosecco sparkling wine is a dry wine, characterized by a brilliant pale yellow colour, with a fine perlage, balanced with the persistence of the mousse.
At the olfactive sense, the wine is characterized by strong floral (white flowers) and fruited (apple, pear, exotic fruits and citrus fruits) points, expressing elegance and finesse. At the taste, it presents itself in balance between soft and hard components, which united with the sapidity, give points of freshness, softness and vivacity at the palate.

Denomination: Rosso di Montalcino
Typology: Red
Region: Tuscany
Degustation: the Rosso di Montalcino is a visually limpid wine, brilliant, red ruby intense coloured. It has a characteristic and intense perfume and a dry, warm and nicely tannic flavour.